£1.50

D1144884

20TH CENTURY MUSIC

20s & 30s

BETWEEN THE WARS

20TH CENTURY MUSIC – '20s & '30s
was produced by

David West 𝘈𝘬 **Children's Books**
7 Princeton Court
55 Felsham Road
London SW15 1AZ

Picture Research: Carrie Haines
Designer: Rob Shone
Editor: James Pickering

First published in Great Britain in 2001 by
Heinemann Library, Halley Court, Jordan Hill,
Oxford OX2 8EJ, a division of Reed Educational and
Professional Publishing Limited.

OXFORD MELBOURNE AUCKLAND
JOHANNESBURG BLANTYRE GABORONE
IBADAN PORTSMOUTH (NH) USA CHICAGO

Copyright © 2001 David West Children's Books

05 04 03 02 01
10 9 8 7 6 5 4 3 2 1

ISBN 0 431 14211 4 (HB)
ISBN 0 431 14218 1 (PB)

British Library Cataloguing in Publication Data

Hayes, Malcolm
The 20s & 30s: between the wars. - (20th century
music)
1. Music - 20th century - Juvenile literature
I. Title II. Nineteen hundred and twenty-forty
780.9'04

Printed and bound in Italy

PHOTO CREDITS :
Abbreviations: t-top, m-middle, b-bottom, r-right,
l-left.

Front cover - m - Lebrecht Collection, br - The
Bridgeman Art Library. 4-5t & b, 7t, 8 all, 9 both, 10t
11 all, 13 t & m, 14, 15 t & bl, 16 both, 17 m, 18
both, 19 tl, 20 tr, 22-23, 23mr, 24b, 24-25, 27 both,
28b, 29m & b - Lebrecht Collection. 3, 12r, 13b, -
Kurt Weill Foundation/Lebrecht Collection. 4l, 5br,
17b, 28r - Mary Evans Picture Library. 5tr, 12l t-b,
15br, 17t, 21br, 23br, 24tr - AKG London. 6tr, 6-7,
26-27 - The Bridgeman Art Library. 6b, 25b - The Art
Archive. 20l - Redferns. 21l & tr, 22 bl, 25t - The
Kobal Collection. 15ml, 22tr, 26bl, 29tl - Hulton
Getty. 26r - The Britten Estate. 19tr - Archivo Manuel
de Falla/Lebrecht Collection. 19b - TL/Lebrecht
Collection.

*Front cover: King Oliver's Creole Jazz Band (main
image), Arnold Schoenberg.*

*The dates in brackets after a person's name
give the years that he or she lived.*

*An explanation of difficult words can be
found in the glossary on page 30.*

20TH CENTURY MUSIC

20s & 30s
BETWEEN THE WARS

Malcolm Hayes

Heinemann
LIBRARY

CONTENTS

KING OLIVER
Joe 'King' Oliver (1885–1938: back row, centre) was one of jazz's great cornet-players. His Creole Jazz Band was a hit in Chicago, and made some brilliant recordings.

NAZISM
Adolf Hitler's National Socialist Party came legally to power in Germany in 1933 after a general election. Hitler quickly transformed the country into a militaristic Fascist state.

NATIONAL HERO
After some years in Paris in the 1920s, Heitor Villa-Lobos (1887–1959) returned to his native Brazil to compose and teach.

5

RE-BUILDING, RE-THINKING

After the First World War (1914–18), the world was a different place. Europe's great empires had fallen apart into exhausted and squabbling nation states, dogged by political instability and mass unemployment. America was tipped by the Wall Street stock market crash of 1929 into economic depression. But the 'Roaring Twenties' were also about having a good time, now that the war was over. Jazz caught the mood perfectly, and swept through America and Europe. Composers, like everyone else, found themselves trying to move on into a strange new age. They responded in different ways. Arnold Schoenberg and his followers explored controversial twelve-note (or 'serial') music. Stravinsky's 'neo-classical' works were inspired by music of the past. And the new influence of jazz on the classical concert hall was led by the genius of George Gershwin.

SWAN-SONG
An illustration from an early recording of Turandot, the last opera of Giacomo Puccini (1858–1924), and also the last opera to have won a regular place on the international circuit.

TWELVE-NOTE MUSIC

There are twelve notes in the chromatic scale of western music. For centuries, composers had been using them in the traditional way. But in his atonal works, Arnold Schoenberg (1874–1951) had already found that his music's harmonic language didn't seem to work in traditional terms any more. So he came up with the 'twelve-note method' (also known as 'serialism').

COUNTING FROM ONE TO TWELVE (IT ISN'T DIFFICULT)

The twelve-note idea had been something waiting to happen – in America, Charles Ives had already experimented with it. Schoenberg developed his own music's chromatic harmony and counterpoint into a working method that would draw these elements together, in a style that was leaner and more sharply focused.

MUSICAL EXPLORER
Schoenberg (pictured here in a self-portrait) once said, 'My music is not modern, it is merely badly played.' He believed in extending the Austro-German musical tradition, not rebelling against it.

THE VIENNA STATE OPERA HOUSE
'Our loathed and beloved Vienna' was how Schoenberg described Austria's music-loving capital city, where the State Opera (formerly the Court Opera) is a proud landmark. The Viennese, however, generally disliked Schoenberg's music.

THE ALPS
For Webern, nature was a central inspiration. He was a keen and expert mountaineer, and also a collector of Alpine flowers, which he took home and planted in his garden in Vienna.

COMPOSING NOTES IN ROWS

The idea is to use note-rows, or 'series', of all twelve notes in order, not repeating a note until the others have also been used – to keep a sense of harmonic and melodic balance. A series can also be used backwards, or upside-down ('inverted'), or both. (This device had been around for centuries: Bach and earlier composers often used it.) Schoenberg said this was like looking at a hat from different angles: 'Whether you see it from the front or sideways or upside-down, you always recognize it as a hat.' This may have been one of Schoenberg's jokes, but there's something in it. Schoenberg composed his first piece to be based entirely on a note-row in July 1921: the Prelude of his Suite for Piano (1920–23).

WEBERN: A LITTLE GOES A LONG WAY

Anton von Webern (1883–1945), a former pupil of Schoenberg, soon found a way of harnessing the twelve-note method to his own, much sparer musical style. The result was a sequence of ultra-concentrated, atmospheric works, including a Symphony for Small Orchestra (1928), a miniature Concerto (1934), and several sets of songs.

MOSES AND AARON
Twelve-note music risks being dry and complex, but a great composer can produce masterpieces with it. Schoenberg never composed the third act of his opera about the Bible story *Moses and Aaron* (1932). But the first two acts work well by themselves, and the music has tremendous dramatic power. At first it was thought too difficult to sing and play, and it was not performed until 1954.

A sculpture of Moses by Michelangelo (1475–1564)

BERG AND OPERA

Like Webern, Alban Berg (1885–1935) was a former pupil of Schoenberg, but his musical personality was very different from theirs. Berg thought in terms of adapting their radical technical ideas to suit his own style, which related more directly to the Romantic tradition of Gustav Mahler (1860–1911).

STORY OF AN UNDERDOG

Woyzeck, by the 19th-century German writer Georg Büchner, was an almost unknown play about a simple-minded, poverty-trapped soldier who struggles to support his girlfriend and their baby son. When she has an affair with a drum-major, Woyzeck kills her and then drowns himself. Berg had been riveted by the play's performance in Vienna. By 1922 he had finished his opera based on it, changing the soldier's name to Wozzeck.

BERG AT HIS DESK
Berg only composed quite a small number of works, but almost all are large-scale and richly detailed, like his Chamber Concerto (1925).

ALMA MAHLER
Mahler's young widow, who later married the architect Walter Gropius, was a strong supporter of the Schoenberg school of composers. Berg dedicated Wozzeck to her.

A SUCCESSFUL MODERNIST
Wozzeck was regularly performed during Berg's lifetime. When Berg died suddenly, Schoenberg wrote to Webern: 'The saddest aspect is – it had to be the one of us who had success.'

Panorama vom Wörthersee und Umgebung
aus der Vogelschau.

A view of the Wörthersee lake in southern Austria. Berg often worked at his Waldhaus ('forest house') nearby.

MANON GROPIUS AND BERG'S VIOLIN CONCERTO

Berg dedicated his Violin Concerto (1935) 'to the memory of an angel'. This was Manon Gropius, the daughter of Berg's friend Alma Mahler (Gustav Mahler's widow) by her second marriage. Manon had died suddenly, and Berg's concerto reflects on her life, death and memory. Before he could hear it performed, Berg himself died of a blood infection.

Manon Gropius, who was only 18 when she died of polio.

A MODERNIST COMPOSER BECOMES WORLD-FAMOUS

Wozzeck's première in Berlin in 1925 had a huge impact (in spite of an abusive newspaper review of this dissonant modern score by 'Alban Berg, a Chinaman from Vienna'). The story is told in tightly constructed and intercut scenes, influenced by the techniques of cinema films of the time. Berg's music strikes a balance between tonal and atonal music. It draws together elements of both, to create a style that was exciting and new.

THE SEAMIER SIDE OF LIFE

Berg began *Lulu*, his second and last opera, in 1929, but did not live to finish it. Based on two plays by the German Frank Wedekind, it traces the downhill path of a *femme fatale* and her various destructive relationships – Lulu eventually meets her death in London, murdered by the notorious Jack the Ripper. The opera uses a version of Schoenberg's twelve-note method as one of many technical devices. After Berg's widow died in 1976, *Lulu* was completed by the Viennese composer Friedrich Cerha (born 1926).

FOLK MUSIC RENEWED

Before the First World War, Hungary's Béla Bartók (1881–1945) and Czechoslovakia's Leos Janáček (1854–1928) had been keen collectors of the folk music of central Europe. By now they had each found ways of developing this in their own music.

BARTOK
Throughout his life, Bartók copied out the folk music he had recorded in Hungary's villages and countryside, often arranging it for the piano.

FOLK MUSICIANS
Bartók greatly admired the inventiveness and energy of Hungarian and Transylvanian folk music.

MODERN DANCING

For Bartók, folk music was something ancient and timeless, yet also vividly alive, which could fuel the development of genuinely modern music. In a sequence of string quartets and piano music, he forged a driving, dissonant, and also exotic musical style, often built out of the tiny melodic fragments that are typical of folk song and dance music. Other major works were his choral *Cantata Profana* (1930) and his orchestral *Music for Strings, Percussion and Celesta* (1936).

HUNGARY SINGS

Zoltán Kodály (1882–1967) responded to folk music with an easygoing, straightforwardly colourful style.

KATYA KABANOVA
Many Czechs resented Russia's powerful presence nearby, but Janáček deeply admired Russian culture. His opera Katya Kabanova *was based on a play by the Russian writer Alexander Ostrovsky.*

VISITING ENGLAND
Janáček had to wait many years for international success, but was proud of it when it came. In England he met the conductor Sir Henry Wood (left), who invited Janáček to his country home near London.

KAMILA STOSSLOVA
'Today I have written down in musical notes my sweetest longings,' wrote Janáček to Kamila Stösslová in February 1928. The music was his passionate Second String Quartet. It was published after his death with the subtitle 'Intimate Letters'. But Janáček himself called it 'Love Letters'.

Kodály's comic opera *Háry János* (1926), about a much-loved rogue of Hungarian legend, was a great success, and so were his orchestral *Peacock Variations* (1939). In the *Psalmus Hungaricus* (1923) for chorus and orchestra, Kodály created a proud national masterpiece.

A LATE LOVE
Now an old man, Janáček was swept up in a growing, yet mostly distant passion for a younger, married woman, Kamila Stösslová. She inspired in him music of blazing intensity, rooted in the style of Czech folk music. This included a sequence of great operas: *Katya Kabanova* (1921), *The Cunning Little Vixen* (or *Vixen Sharp-Ears*, 1924), *The Makropoulos Case* (1926), and *From the House of the Dead* (1927). Other masterpieces are the Sinfonietta (1926) for orchestra and the *Glagolitic Mass* (1926), a powerful choral setting of the Mass service in the old Czech language.

Kamila Stösslová inspired the last work Janáček would complete, his Second String Quartet.

FROM SOCIAL COMMITMENT TO SOCIALISM

Germany's First World War defeat led to the foundation of the Weimar Republic (named after the German town). Life became desperately hard. Germany was reduced to poverty, very high inflation and mass unemployment by the peace terms of the victorious powers, Britain, France and Italy. Political extremism flourished – and the result was the rise to power of Adolf Hitler and his National Socialist (Nazi) Party in 1933.

LOTTE LENYA
Weill and Lenya first met in 1922. She became a famous singer-actress both in Weill's stage works and in films.

MUSIC FROM HARD TIMES

Kurt Weill (1900–50), the son of a Jewish cantor, caused a stir with his early Violin Concerto (1924). His style, influenced both by Schoenberg and Stravinsky, sounded more modern than earlier music. But Weill was sharply aware of the appalling conditions around him in Germany. He simplified and sharpened his music's language, broadening its popular appeal, and worked with the left-wing German playwright, Bertolt Brecht (1898–1956). A sequence of theatre works followed, revealing Weill as a great songwriter: they include *The Threepenny Opera* (1928) and *Happy End* (1929).

PROPAGANDA
Among these posters are a pro-Nazi one proclaiming 'Our last hope – Hitler' (many Germans agreed). Another calls Nazism and Communism 'enemies of democracy'.

12

FROM BERLIN TO BROADWAY (VIA PARIS)

Weill then collaborated with the German writer Georg Kaiser (1878–1945) on the theatre work *Silverlake* (1933). When Hitler's Nazis came to power and instantly banned it, Weill escaped from Germany and moved to Paris. There he met up again with his then ex-wife, the singer Lotte Lenya, and Brecht. Together they created *The Seven Deadly Sins* (1933), which mixes song and ballet. Weill and Lenya crossed in 1935 to America, where they remarried, and Weill wrote his first Broadway shows: *Johnny Johnson* (1936) and *Knickerbocker Holiday* (1938).

EISLER: MORE A HARD-LINER

Hanns Eisler (1899–1962), who studied under Schoenberg, also started out as an angry young modernist. But his Marxist political beliefs led him also to write music for audiences and performers outside 'middle class' places like the classical concert hall. He composed songs for cabaret theatres, workers' choirs, and Berlin bars. Eisler, too, fled from Hitler's Germany and moved to America in 1938.

KURT WEILL
When this photograph was taken in 1929, Weill's theatre works were already famous throughout the whole of Europe.

COMPOSER WITH A CONSCIENCE

Paul Hindemith (1895–1963) felt that a composer had a moral duty to widen classical music's involvement in society. He wrote music for schools and amateurs as well as for professionals. Hindemith's opera *Mathis der Maler* (Matthias the Painter, 1934) is about a medieval German artist's commitment to his work in a hostile world. It was banned in Germany, and first performed in Switzerland in 1938.

Hindemith playing the viola

WEILL AND BRECHT
The composer and the playwright sometimes quarrelled, but on the whole they collaborated brilliantly. These pictures were taken in Berlin in 1928, between rehearsals for the première of The Threepenny Opera.

PARIS, STRAVINSKY AND NEO-CLASSICISM

STRAVINSKY AND COLLEAGUES

Stravinsky was the most famous classical composer of his day, and he knew many of the world's great artists. Composing so often for the theatre meant that he became personal friends with writers (such as Jean Cocteau) and painters (such as Pablo Picasso) as well as musicians and conductors, many of them living or working in Paris. Stravinsky also travelled far and wide as a concert pianist.

From left: Jean Cocteau, Picasso, Stravinsky, Olga Picasso, Picasso's wife at the time, in 1926

With the First World War over, Paris soon recovered its form as a magnet for artists everywhere. The colourful, international musical scene was dominated by Igor Stravinsky (1882–1971). Exiled from his native Russia, Stravinsky started a new life as a French citizen.

DANCING ON

The ballet *Pulcinella* (1920) was the first of Stravinsky's rediscoveries of the musical past. It was commissioned by his pre-war colleague, the Russian impresario Sergei Diaghilev (1872–1929). *Pulcinella* adapts music by 18th-century Italian composers (including Pergolesi) in a brilliantly individual way. The style, known as 'neo-classical', is both expressive and distant. Stravinsky produced more ballet masterpieces in *Apollon Musagète* (Apollo, Leader of the Muses, 1928) and *Perséphone* (1933), whose principal dancer also narrates the story from Ancient Greece. And the *Symphony of Psalms* (1930) for chorus and orchestra is one of his greatest works.

RAVEL: CHILDHOOD AND JAZZ

Maurice Ravel (1875–1937), too, was producing some of his finest music. *L'Enfant et les Sortilèges* (The Child and the Sprites, 1925) is a one-act opera about a naughty child who learns better behaviour from the fairy-tale characters in his books and the animals in his parents' garden. It uses the sounds of folk drumming and 1920s dances. Ravel's orchestral *Boléro* (1928), influenced by jazz and Spanish dance-rhythms, became an instant classic.

MARTINU
Czechoslovakia's Bohuslav Martinu (1890–1959) came to live in Paris in 1923. There he wrote music which was often on Czech subjects (like his Field Mass *of 1939), and sometimes also flirted with jazz and neo-classicism.*

PARIS BETWEEN THE WARS
For artists from all over Europe and America, Paris was the place to be. The writers Ernest Hemingway and James Joyce, and the painter and sculptor Pablo Picasso all lived there for a time.

OPERA RUSSE
The fashion in Paris for everything Russian continued after the war. Stravinsky's Mavra *(1922) and his opera-oratorio* Oedipus Rex *(1927) were both premièred there.*

SACRED SOUNDS

In 1928, Olivier Messiaen (1908–92) attracted attention with a short organ work, *Le Banquet Céleste* (The Celestial Banquet). Its rich sound and religious theme were striking. His next works included a set of piano *Préludes* (1929), the orchestral *L'Ascension* (1933), and the organ cycle *La Nativité du Seigneur* (The Nativity of our Lord, 1935).

AT THE ORGAN
Messiaen played the organ at Mass every Sunday at the Church of Sainte-Trinité in Paris.

GREAT CONSERVATIVES

Composers tend to react less to the musical world around them as they get older. Some have been accused of living in a comfortable bygone age in their later works. But in fact they were enriching the present in their own way.

THE LANDSCAPE STILL SPEAKS

Already a star in his native Finland, Jean Sibelius (1865–1957) became an international celebrity. Fame comes at a price, and Sibelius found it harder to create works that lived up to everyone's expectations. Two of his last and greatest achievements were the Sixth and Seventh Symphonies (1923 and 1924). And there was the magnificent symphonic poem *Tapiola* (1926), depicting his country's forest landscapes (Tapio was the forest god of Finnish legend). Tortured by self-doubt, Sibelius almost certainly completed an Eighth Symphony. Then he destroyed it.

HOME LIFE
Richard Strauss is pictured here with his wife, Pauline – a gifted soprano singer – and their young son, Franz. When not working hard at his composing, Strauss was a keen card-player.

NORTHERN TALENT
Besides Sibelius (standing second from right), this picture, taken at the Nordic Music Festival, shows Sweden's Wilhelm Stenhammar (1871–1927, seated left) and Denmark's Carl Nielsen (1865–1931, seated right).

OPERAS – AND MORE OPERAS

Richard Strauss (1864–1949) was the one-time young lion of German music. Now, living in his beautiful mountain home in Bavaria, and composing in the masterly, conservative style that suited him, he got involved as little as he could in Germany's political and social upheavals going on around him. He wrote a long sequence of operas, including *Intermezzo* (1924), about a quarrel between himself and his wife; *Arabella*, set in 19th-century Vienna; and *Daphne*, a story from Ancient Greece.

A RUSSIAN EXILE

Having left Russia after the Revolution, Sergei Rachmaninov (1873–1943) never returned. He lived mainly in New York and Switzerland, and toured America and Europe as one of the greatest ever concert pianists. Rachmaninov composed only six works in these years, but they are all very important. They include a Fourth Piano Concerto (1926) and the brilliant *Rhapsody on a Theme of Paganini* (1934) for piano and orchestra; a Third Symphony (1936); and the *Symphonic Dances* (1940), a fourth symphony in all but name.

QUIET MASTERY
Gabriel Fauré (1845–1924) retired from teaching in his old age, but kept on composing. His beautiful late chamber works include a Piano Trio (1923) and a String Quartet (1924).

COUNTRY COMPOSER
On the proceeds of his earlier operas, Puccini built his country home at Torre del Lago in Tuscany. When he was there, he always used to compose while wearing a hat!

TURANDOT
Giacomo Puccini (1858–1924) decided that all his earlier operas were, so he said, no more than *un burletta* (a pantomime). He set about composing *Turandot*, based on a Chinese legend about a cold-hearted princess who eventually yields to love. Although Puccini died before finishing the closing scene, *Turandot* is his grandest, greatest, and most colourful work. It was completed by the Italian composer Franco Alfano (1875–1954).

An illustration from 1926

LOCAL COLOUR

Nationalist feeling in the music of countries around the world was proudly reflected. Composers in countries as far apart as Brazil and Poland aimed to create a national style, which would also have the strength and quality to be successful abroad.

DENMARK'S MUSICAL VOICE

Like Sibelius, the Dane Carl Nielsen (1865–1931) was a leading Nordic composer. Amongst his most ambitious works was his Fifth Symphony, which he wrote in 1922. Nielsen also wrote chamber and piano music, and songs for school choirs. His cantata *Springtime on Funen* (1921) celebrated the Danish island where he was born. The lean, unexaggerated style of Nielsen's music has come to be regarded as typically Danish, although it was not directly based on folk music.

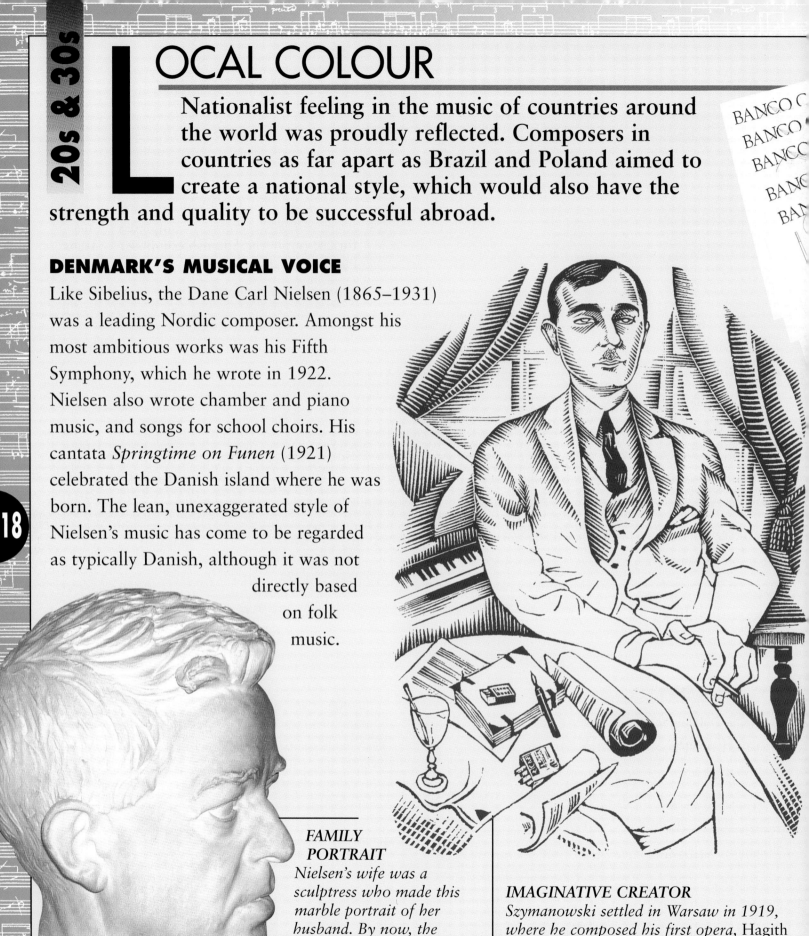

FAMILY PORTRAIT
Nielsen's wife was a sculptress who made this marble portrait of her husband. By now, the composer had risen from humble beginnings to international fame.

IMAGINATIVE CREATOR
Szymanowski settled in Warsaw in 1919, where he composed his first opera, Hagith *(1922). From 1927 to 1932 he directed the Warsaw Conservatory of Music. His early death was caused by tuberculosis.*

18

TRUE CELEBRITY
Villa-Lobos was famous enough to appear on one of Brazil's bank notes.

MANUEL DE FALLA
Two great inspirations for Manuel de Falla (1876–1946) were Spanish folk music, and Spain's golden age of classical music in the 16th century. From 1926, Falla worked on *Atlántida* (Atlantis), a huge oratorio about Spain's destiny as the nation that discovered the Americas. He died leaving it unfinished. A version was eventually completed by his former pupil, the Spanish composer Ernesto Halffter (1905–89).

Falla (left) with the Russian dancer Leonidé Massine on a visit to the Alhambra Palace in Granada, Spain.

BRAZILIAN CARNIVAL

Brazil produced a major composer in Heitor Villa-Lobos (1887–1959). He visited Paris in the 1920s and then returned to Rio de Janeiro to conduct, teach, and compose over 2,000 works, combining the energy of Brazilian street bands with the methods of western classical music. His nine *Bachianas Brasileiras* – including one for soprano voice and eight cellos – blend the style of Brazilian folk music with the technical devices of Bach.

POLISH ADVENTURES

Poland's Karol Szymanowski (1882–1937) visited Italy and north Africa, and this inspired the unusual, exotic sounds in his early works. His opera *King Roger* (1926) is set in medieval Sicily, and explores the conflict between the King's Christian faith and the pagan influence of a mysterious, god-like visitor disguised as a shepherd. Szymanowski then became interested in the folk music of Poland's Tatra mountains, whose sounds and rhythms influenced his choral *Stabat Mater* (1926) and his ballet *Harnasie* (1935).

THE TANGO
By the 1920s, Latin America's favourite dance was being enjoyed all over the world.

JAZZ AND MUSICALS

Jazz caught the mood of the times. America wanted to cheer itself up during the Great Depression, and Europe was determined to enjoy itself after the First World War. Gramophone records and broadcast radio brought the jazz age into almost every home, while the change from silent movies to 'talkies' led to huge new audiences for musicals on the silver screen.

STAR CLARINETTIST
Benny Goodman was one of the first to take jazz into the classical concert hall, including a legendary Carnegie Hall concert in New York City, in 1938.

JAZZ: AN ERA OF GREAT ARTISTS

The piano-playing of Jelly Roll Morton (1890–1941) was the talk of Chicago; Louis Armstrong ('Satchmo', 1900–71) mesmerized New York with his trumpet-playing and vocals (and invented 'scat', an improvised vocal technique of imitating instruments). Count Basie (1904–84) and Paul Whiteman (1890–1967) steered jazz towards the 1930s big bands of clarinettist Benny Goodman (1909–86) and trombonist Glenn Miller (1904–44). Duke Ellington (1899–1974) expanded the scope of jazz numbers, paving the way for his trademark 'symphonic jazz', and also proved himself a sensitive and imaginative pianist. The sophisticated cornet and piano of Bix Beiderbecke (1903–31) pointed towards the future age of modern jazz, while the piano virtuosity of Art Tatum (1909–56) amazed everyone.

LOUIS ARMSTRONG
In 1924, 'Satchmo' moved from Chicago to New York, where his reputation grew as one of jazz's greatest ever trumpet players.

A LEGEND IS BORN
Show Boat opened in New York in 1927. The next year the bass singer Paul Robeson (1898–1976) appeared in its London première, singing 'Ol' Man River'.

EUROPE JOINS IN

In England, jazz influenced *Façade* (1922), an 'entertainment' for reciter and instruments by the young William Walton (1902–83). France's Maurice Ravel (1875–1937) imitated jazz melodies and rhythms in his two Piano Concertos (1930 and 1931). Violinist Stéphane Grappelli (1908–97) and guitarist Django Reinhardt (1910–53) founded the Quintette du Hot Club de France in 1934.

THE BROADWAY MUSICAL LIGHTS UP THE WORLD

Jerome Kern (1885–1945) and Oscar Hammerstein II (1895–1960) produced a classic musical in *Show Boat* (1927), with its rich spectacle of songs, story and dance. The music and lyrics of Cole Porter (1891–1964) sparkled in *The Gay Divorce* (1932) and *Anything Goes* (1934). And Hollywood lavished its resources on the screen musical. *Show Boat* was first filmed in 1929. The songs of Irving Berlin (1888–1989) graced *Top Hat* (1935) and *Follow the Fleet* (1936). And Gershwin, a master of the Broadway show (see pp. 22–23), produced a rip-roaring score for *Shall We Dance?* (1937).

AL JOLSON AS THE JAZZ SINGER

Born Asa Yoelsen in Lithuania, Al Jolson (1885–1950) wowed Broadway audiences throughout the 1920s with his stage magnetism and his trademark phrase: 'You ain't heard nothin' yet!' When Warner Brothers made one of its first 'talkie' movies, *The Jazz Singer*, in 1927, Jolson starred in the title role. It was a massive success – and the film musical was born.

Al Jolson successfully managed to move from stage to screen.

21

THE DUKE
From 1927, Duke Ellington's growing fame as a pianist, composer and arranger was spread by his band's broadcasts from the Cotton Club in New York City.

AMERICA AND AMERICAS

Fired up by the excitement of the jazz age, American music began to bring fresh life and energy to the classical tradition, producing an original genius in George Gershwin (1899–1937). Gershwin did much more than merely 'cross over' the boundaries between popular and classical music. His achievement was to enrich both worlds equally.

GERSHWIN: SONGS, SHOWS AND OPERA

Gershwin grew up listening to classical music, as well as popular songs and jazz. In 1919, he wrote his first hit song, 'Swanee'. More songs poured from him, many – like 'The Man I Love' – with lyrics by his brother Ira (1896–1983). His theatre successes on New York's Broadway included *Lady, Be Good!* (1924), *Oh, Kay!* (1926), *Strike Up the Band* (1927) and *Girl Crazy* (1930).

THE ALL-ROUNDER
Writing, composing, directing, and often also appearing in his own musicals, George M. Cohan (1878–1942) created Little Nellie Kelly, The Rise of Rosie O'Reilly, The Merry Malones *and* Billie.

FRED AND GINGER
Fred Astaire (1899–1987) and Ginger Rogers (1911–95) starred in George and Ira Gershwin's scintillating screen musical Shall We Dance? *(1937).*

Gershwin also dazzled audiences with *Rhapsody in Blue* (1924) for piano and jazz band or orchestra (commissioned by Paul Whiteman) and the Piano Concerto (1925). In *Porgy and Bess* (1935) he created a great American opera: among the songs sung by its black cast are 'Summertime' and 'It Ain't Necessarily So'. Tragically, he died from a brain tumour when he was only in his thirties.

COPLAND: FROM JAZZ TO THE PRAIRIE

Like Gershwin, Aaron Copland (1900–90) was born to Russian Jewish parents in New York. There are jazz elements to his Piano Concerto (1926), while the Piano Variations (1930) are a masterpiece of Copland's concise, 'serious' style. He also wrote music aimed at broad popular appeal: *El Salón México* (1936) for orchestra, and a ballet about America's legendary outlaw, *Billy the Kid* (1940).

MUSIC OF THE FUTURE

Destroying his earlier works, Edgar Varèse (1883–1965) had moved from France to New York in 1915, hoping to discover new worlds of sound. His dissonant *Amériques* (Americas, 1921) even includes the sound of traffic sirens.

BILLY THE KID
Copland used several cowboy songs in his ballet, including 'Git Along Little Dogie'.

A Gershwin hit from 1927

THE GERSHWINS
The brilliant working collaboration of George (left) and Ira Gershwin (right) continued through to Porgy and Bess (where Ira was co-lyricist with DuBose Heyward) and Shall We Dance?

SOVIET RUSSIA

After the Russian Revolution of 1917, the Communist Party gradually increased its hold on the country's life. At first, composers were allowed to be radical and experimental. This changed sharply when Joseph Stalin took power in the mid-1920s.

RUTHLESS LEADER
Lenin and his Bolshevik Party at first struggled to hold on to political power in Russia, but gradually won the upper hand, and took power of the new Soviet Union.

THE MACHINE AGE

Revolutionary Russia was supposed to be leading its people into a new, industrial age of political and social equality. This official line was echoed in the heavy, pounding rhythms of *Steel* (1928), a ballet by Alexander Mosolov (1900–73). But the biggest star of the new Soviet Union was Dmitri Shostakovich (1906–75). He completed his First Symphony in 1925, and it was soon played all over the world.

BRILLIANT NEWCOMER
The First Symphony of Shostakovich (right, sitting at the piano) was one of musical history's most amazing débuts. Aged just 19, the composer had produced a remarkably mature masterpiece.

EISENSTEIN AND PROKOFIEV

Prokofiev (left) and the film director Eisenstein worked closely together. In places, Eisenstein devised his filming to fit the music, rather than the other way round.

PROKOFIEV'S ALEXANDER NEVSKY

In 1938, the Russian film director Sergei Eisenstein (1898–1948) made his film *Alexander Nevsky*. This was a patriotic story about the winner of a great battle on a frozen lake, against an invading army of medieval knights. Prokofiev composed one of the greatest of all film scores, and then re-worked the music as a cantata for chorus and orchestra.

Alexander Nevsky was a real-life Russian hero. The Russian Church declared him a saint in 1547.

SOVIET NIGHTMARE

In 1936, Stalin saw a performance of Shostakovich's new opera, *Lady Macbeth of the Mtsensk District*. Disgusted by its story of adultery, murder and suicide, and not appreciating the music's lurid brilliance, Stalin authorized a vicious newspaper attack on Shostakovich. The composer withdrew the opera (he later revised it as *Katerina Ismailova*) and his Fourth Symphony (1936). With political repression at its height, Shostakovich feared for his life. His much less radical Fifth Symphony (1937) restored his official reputation. But he composed no more operas.

THE WANDERER RETURNS

Sergei Prokofiev (1891–1953) had been living in Europe and America as a composer-pianist in exile. His return in 1936 was badly timed. The Soviet authorities wanted music about 'socialist realism', and disliked the radical side of Prokofiev's style. But he scored hits with his children's entertainment *Peter and the Wolf* (1936), and his ballet *Romeo and Juliet* (1938).

CONSTRUCTIVISM

Experimental art was an officially approved part of cultural life in early Soviet Russia.

ВЛАДИМИР МАЯКОВСКИЙ

BRITAIN AND BRITTEN

During the 1920s and 1930s, English music was looking both forwards and backwards. Ralph Vaughan Williams (1872–1958) was building on his earlier involvement in English folk song. And a rising new star, Benjamin Britten (1913–76), was eagerly spreading his musical wings.

MORE THAN JUST A DREAM OF ENGLAND

Vaughan Williams served in the army throughout the First World War. Afterwards, in 1921, he produced two deeply felt masterpieces, as if quietly remembering the millions who had died: these were *A Pastoral Symphony* ('not really lambkins frisking at all,' said the composer) and a chamber opera, *The Shepherds of the Delectable Mountains*. Other works were *Job* (1931), a ballet based on the biblical story; a Fourth Symphony (1934); and *Serenade to Music* (1938) for 16 solo singers and an orchestra.

BRITTEN AND AUDEN
In his cantata Our Hunting Fathers *(1936), Britten (right) set words by the radical poet W.H. Auden.*

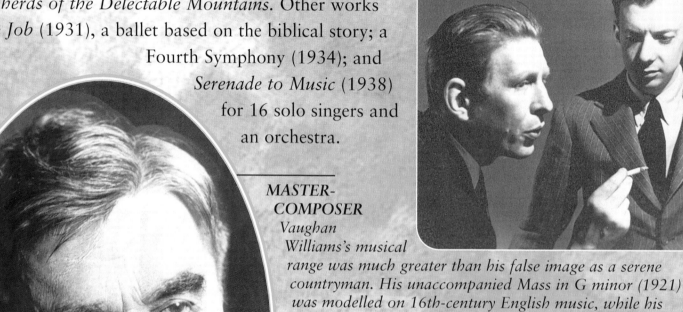

MASTER-COMPOSER
Vaughan Williams's musical range was much greater than his false image as a serene countryman. His unaccompanied Mass in G minor (1921) was modelled on 16th-century English music, while his Fourth Symphony (1935) is full of dissonance.

DREAM-LANDSCAPE

The English often prefer the idea of an imaginary countryside to the real thing. Vaughan Williams preferred living in London.

WALTON TRIUMPHS

The great American violinist Jascha Heifetz (1901–87) commissioned a Violin Concerto from Walton, who in 1939 came up with a lyrical and colourful masterpiece.

THE NEW GENERATION

After causing an early stir with *Façade* (1922), William Walton (1902–83) made his name with his Viola Concerto (1929), the oratorio *Belshazzar's Feast* (1931), a First Symphony (1935) and a Violin Concerto (1939). His music blended an individual style of English lyrical beauty with snappy, driving rhythms. Michael Tippett (1905–98) came to prominence with his elegant, lively Concerto for Double String Orchestra (1939).

BRITTEN: A SPECTACULAR TALENT

Britten's tight-reined, yet approachable musical style combined a fluent composing technique with a boldly original cast of mind. He had early success with the *Variations on a Theme of Frank Bridge* for string orchestra (1937), a tribute to the English composer who had taught him. Like Tippett, Britten was a lifelong pacifist. When the Second World War loomed, he left England for America. There, in 1939, he composed his darkly troubled Violin Concerto and a vivid, brilliant song cycle, *Les Illuminations*, setting words by the French poet Artur Rimbaud (1854–91).

ELGAR AT ABBEY ROAD STUDIOS

After the death of his wife in 1920, Edward Elgar (1857–1934) did not complete another major work. Instead he conducted recordings of his music, including his Violin Concerto (1910) with the 16-year-old Yehudi Menuhin. Elgar also sketched out parts of a planned Third Symphony. In 1997, these were 'elaborated' into a complete version by the English composer Anthony Payne (born 1936).

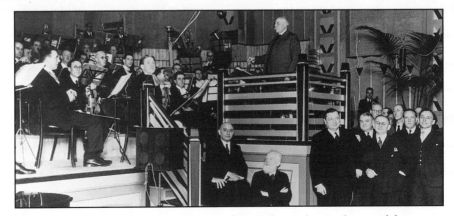

Elgar conducts at the opening of London's legendary Abbey Road recording studios, in 1931. The Irish writer George Bernard Shaw is sitting with his arms folded, below Elgar.

28

FASCISM: COMPOSERS REACT

Some composers approved of the rise of extreme right-wing Fascist power in Germany and Italy. Some did not, but felt they should stay and support their country's cultural values. Others left – in protest, or in fear for their lives, or both.

ITALY: A MIXED RESPONSE

The Italian dictator Benito Mussolini found an admirer in Pietro Mascagni (1863–1945), as famous as ever for his opera *Cavalleria Rusticana* (Rustic Chivalry, 1889). Mascagni composed *Nerone* (1935), about the Roman emperor Nero, in tribute. Ottorino Respighi (1879–1936) wrote two sumptuous symphonic poems, *The Pines of Rome* (1924) and *Roman Festivals* (1924), which share something of Italian Fascism's pride in the national past. But Alfredo Casella (1883–1947) and Gian Francesco Malipiero (1882–1973) were only interested in their country's musical past.

The 1936 Winter and Summer Olympics were held in Germany.

HITLER AND THE WAGNER LEGACY
The element of German nationalism in Wagner's operas was seized on by Hitler, pictured here at the Wagner Festival at Bayreuth with the composer's grandson, Wieland Wagner (right) and Wieland's English-born mother, Winifred Wagner.

Luigi Dallapiccola (1904–75), the composer of the more modernist opera *Volo di Notte* (Night Flight, 1940), took a strongly anti-Fascist position.

STRAUSS COMPROMISES

Hitler's rise to power in 1933 put Richard Strauss in a difficult position. He was an old man and wanted a quiet life, but he was also Germany's most senior composer and a celebrity.

MASCAGNI IN BERLIN
Identifying with German and Italian Fascism, Pietro Mascagni (1863–1945) visited Berlin, and composed his last opera Nerone *in admiration of Mussolini. His music was boycotted by other Italian musicians at home and abroad.*

RESPIGHI IN ROME
Respighi, who had settled in Rome, was not a committed supporter of Fascism, but his interest in Italy's musical past influenced his dramatic cantata Lauda per la Natività del Signore *(Praise of Our Lord's Nativity, 1930).*

THE 1936 GERMAN OLYMPICS
The 1936 Olympic Games in Germany were used by the Nazi Party as a thinly disguised opportunity to promote Hitler's ideas about the superiority of white races, especially the 'Aryan' German one. In the famous documentary film of the Summer Games in Berlin, made by the German director Leni Riefenstahl (born 1902), the opening ceremony features a choral 'Olympic Hymn'. Its composer was Richard Strauss.

PRINCIPLED RESISTANCE
Dallapiccola's anti-Fascist stand meant that he effectively had to live in hiding for many years.

Therefore a quiet life was impossible. Also, Strauss had a Jewish daughter-in-law to protect (which he successfully did). So he obliged with official demands, while not openly supporting Hitler. But his decision to stay on in Germany was viewed with suspicion by composers who left.

EXODUS

In March 1933, the 'serialist' composer Schoenberg was teaching at Berlin's Prussian Academy of Arts. Its director announced that Hitler was determined 'to break the Jewish stranglehold on Western music'. Schoenberg stormed out. Soon after, he moved with his family to America. By 1940, Hindemith, Weill, Bartók and Stravinsky had all joined him. Europe's loss was American music's gain.

GLOSSARY

ATONALITY A term meaning 'music in no key', often used about the music of Schoenberg and his followers.

CANTATA 'Something sung', so a musical work using voices.

CELESTA An orchestral keyboard instrument with a delicate, silvery sound.

CHAMBER MUSIC Music for a group of solo players.

CHROMATIC Using extreme harmonic language, relating to the twelve-note western scale.

CONCERTO A work for solo instruments and orchestra.

COUNTERPOINT The art of organizing two or more different melodic lines.

DISSONANT (or 'discordant') Notes which, when played together, sound more unstable than classical music is comfortable with.

IMPROVISED Music which is not written down, but composed at the moment it is performed.

KEY The bedrock idea of classical music, where the harmony sounds fixed to a particular 'keynote'.

NEO-CLASSICAL Music which, though contemporary, is based on a style from the past.

ORATORIO A setting of a text on a religious subject, for solo voices, chorus and orchestra.

SINFONIETTA Literally a 'little symphony', but sometimes a large work like Janáček's.

STABAT MATER A medieval Latin poem about the Virgin Mary's grief at the crucifixion of Christ.

STRING QUARTET A work for four stringed instruments: two violins, viola and cello. Also the group that plays it.

SUITE A collection of separate instrumental pieces.

SYMPHONIC POEM A work for orchestra, usually in a single movement (or section), telling a story or depicting a particular scene (say in a city or the countryside).

SYMPHONY Traditionally, an orchestral work in four movements, but it can be expanded to include extra movements and solo and choral voices. There are also one-movement symphonies, like Sibelius's Seventh.

30

WORLD EVENTS

- American women over 21 allowed to vote — 19
- Tuberculosis vaccine discovered — 19
- Creation of Irish Free State — 19
- Hitler's attempt to seize power in Germany — 19
- Stalin takes power in the Soviet Union — 19
- First television pictures transmitted — 19
- Mussolini creates a one-party state in Italy — 19
- Lindbergh flies solo across the Atlantic — 19
- Penicillin discovered by Alexander Fleming — 19
- The Wall Street stockmarket crash — 19
- First football World Cup competition held — 19
- Japan invades Chinese province of Manchuria — 19
- Franklin D. Roosevelt elected US President — 19
- Hitler takes power in Germany — 19
- Dust Bowl destroys American farmland — 19
- Mussolini's Italian army invades Ethiopia — 19
- The Olympic Games are held in Germany — 19
- Japan invades China — 19
- Nuclear fission discovered — 19
- Start of Second World War — 19

TIMELINE

	MUSICAL EVENTS	THE ARTS	FAMOUS MUSICIANS	MUSICAL WORKS
20	•Duke Ellington leads various small bands	•Dadaism: anti-art Dada Fair held in Berlin	•Birth of Charlie 'Bird' Parker, jazz saxophonist	•Pulcinella, ballet with voices by Stravinsky
21	•Schoenberg's first serial works	•Rudolf Valentino stars in the silent film The Sheik	•Death of Engelbert Humperdinck, composer	•Prokofiev's opera The Love of Three Oranges
22	•Première of Janáček's Katya Kabanova	•James Joyce's novel Ulysses published in Paris	•Birth of jazz bass-player Charles Mingus	•Nielsen's Fifth Symphony
23	•Sibelius's Sixth Symphony performed	•W.B. Yeats awarded Nobel Prize for Literature	•Deaths of composers Fauré and Puccini	•Stravinsky's Les Noces
24	•First performance of Schoenberg's Erwartung	•E.M. Forster's novel A Passage to India published	•Louis Armstrong finds fame in New York	•Sibelius's Seventh Symphony
25	•Berg's opera Wozzeck premièred in Berlin	•Sergei Eisenstein's film Battleship Potemkin	•Birth of Miles Davis, jazz trumpeter and composer	•Alban Berg's Chamber Concerto
26	•Première of Janáček's Glagolitic Mass	•Fritz Lang's futuristic film Metropolis	•Fats Waller and Bessie Smith tour together	•Sibelius's Tapiola •Jerome Kern's Show Boat
27	•Stravinsky's Oedipus Rex premièred	•Al Jolson stars in the film musical The Jazz Singer		•Janáček's opera From the House of the Dead
28	•Weill and Brecht's The Threepenny Opera	•Publication of Decline and Fall by Evelyn Waugh	•Birth of Beverly Sills, American opera soprano	•Janáček composes 'Intimate letters'
29	•Kern's Show Boat filmed	•Novel All Quiet on the Western Front published	•Cab Calloway leads the Alabamians jazz band	•Walton's Viola Concerto •Webern's Quartet Op. 22
30	•Première of Gershwin's Girl Crazy on Broadway	•Greta Garbo makes her first talking movie	•Death of Bix Beiderbecke, trumpeter	•Bartók's Cantata Profana
31	•Première of Shostakovich's The Bolt	•James Cagney stars in A Public Enemy	•Death of John Philip Sousa, American composer	•Walton's oratorio Belshazzar's Feast
32	•Gershwin's The Gay Divorce staged	•Aldous Huxley's Brave New World published	•Schoenberg leaves Germany for America	•Schoenberg's opera Moses and Aaron
33	•Louis Armstrong tours Europe	•Release of the first film version of King Kong	•Birth of Marilyn Horne, mezzo-soprano	•Stravinsky's 'sung ballet' Perséphone
34	•Gershwin's show Anything Goes staged	•School of American Ballet founded	•Death of Alban Berg	•Vaughan Williams's Fourth Symphony
35	•Astaire and Rogers star in the musical Top Hat	•The first Penguin paperback books appear	•Birth of English singer Tommy Steele	•Gershwin's opera Porgy and Bess
36	•Prokofiev's Peter and the Wolf is a big hit	•Charlie Chaplin stars in his film Modern Times	•Death of Ravel	•Britten's cantata Our Hunting Fathers
37	•NBC Symphony Orchestra created	•Picasso paints his famous Guernica	•Death of George Gershwin	•Shostakovich's Fifth Symphony
38	•Prokofiev's Romeo and Juliet first performed	•Orson Welles broadcasts The War of the Worlds	•Birth of jazz trumpeter Freddie Hubbard	•Webern's String Quartet, Op. 28
39		•Film of Gone with the Wind released	•Stravinsky moves to America	•Walton's Violin Concerto

INDEX